I0815361

Intro to German

Bela Davis

Deutsch

Abdo Kids Junior
is an Imprint of Abdo Kids
abdobooks.com

Abdo
INTRO TO LANGUAGE
Kids

abdobooks.com

Published by Abdo Kids, a division of ABDO, P.O. Box 398166, Minneapolis, Minnesota 55439.

Printed in China

102023

012024

THIS BOOK CONTAINS RECYCLED MATERIALS

Consultant: Fritzi Knipping

Photo Credits: Getty Images, Shutterstock

Production Contributors: Teddy Borth, Jennie Forsberg, Grace Hansen

Design Contributors: Candice Keimig, Colleen McLaren

Library of Congress Control Number: 2023937673

Publisher's Cataloging-in-Publication Data

Names: Davis, Bela, author.

Title: Intro to German / by Bela Davis

Description: Minneapolis, Minnesota : Abdo Kids, 2024 | Series: Intro to language | Includes online resources and index.

Identifiers: ISBN 9781098268305 (lib. bdg.) | ISBN 9781098269005 (ebook) | ISBN 9781098269357 (Read-to-Me ebook)

Subjects: LCSH: German language--Juvenile literature. | Informal language learning--Juvenile literature. | Language and languages--Juvenile literature. | Bilingual books--Juvenile literature.

Classification: DDC 418.00--dc23

Table of Contents

Intro to German

German is spoken around the world. Let's learn some words!

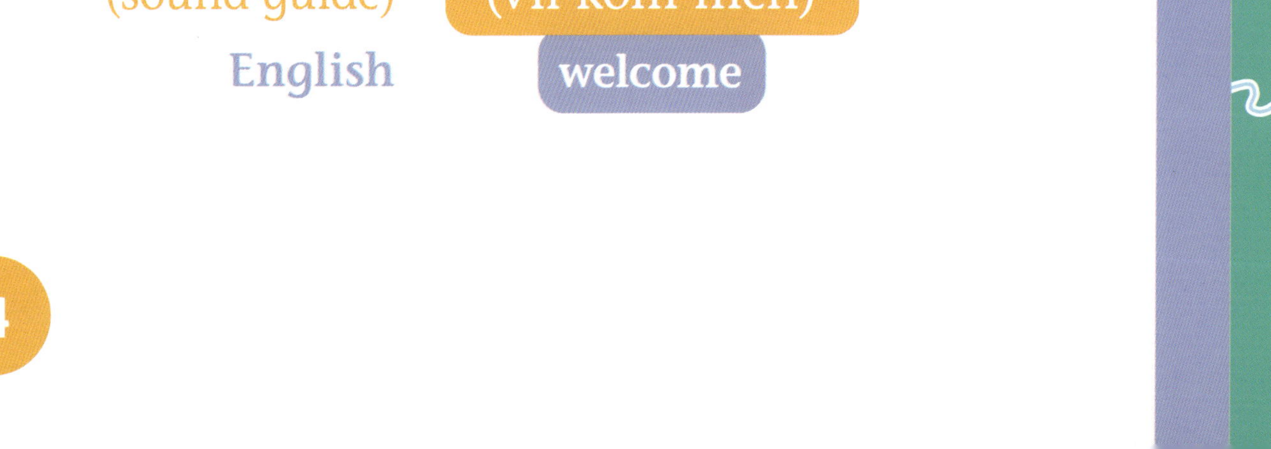

Europe
Germany
Belgium
Luxembourg
Austria
Switzerland
Liechtenstein
N
W
E
S
German is an official language

eins
(ains)
one

zwei
(tsvai)
two

sechs
(zehks)
six

sieben
(zeeben)
seven

drei
(drai)
three

vier
(feer)
four

fünf
(foonf)
five

acht
(ahkt)
eight

neun
(noin)
nine

zehn
(tsen)
ten

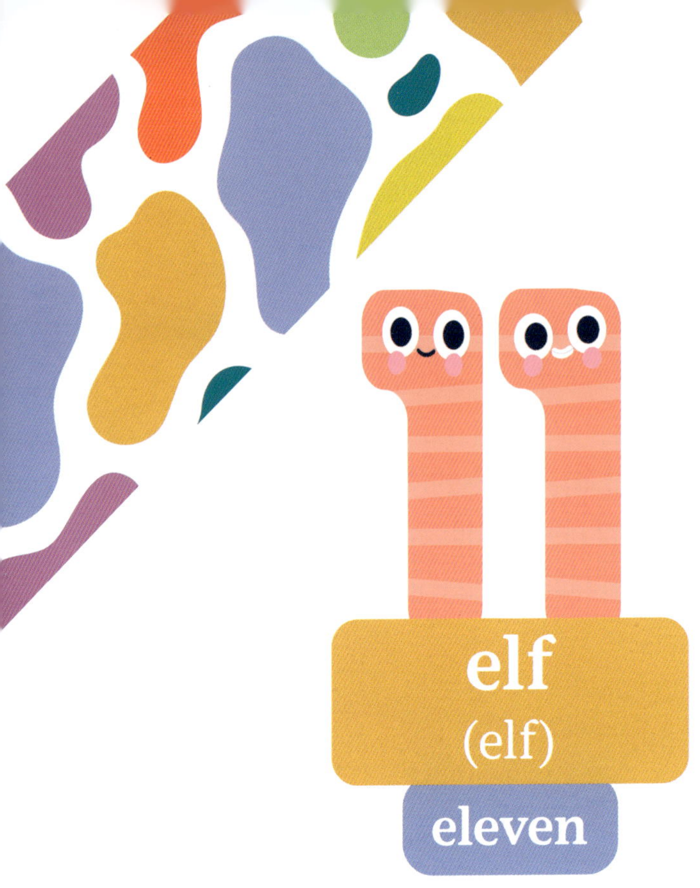
elf
(elf)
eleven

zwölf
(tsvelf)
twelve

sechzehn
(zehks•tsen)
sixteen

siebzehn
(zeeb•tsen)
seventeen

dreizehn
(drai•tsen)
thirteen

vierzehn
(feer•tsen)
fourteen

fünfzehn
(foonf•tsen)
fifteen

achtzehn
(ahkt•tsen)
eighteen

neunzehn
(noin•tsen)
nineteen

zwanzig
(tsvan•tsig)
twenty

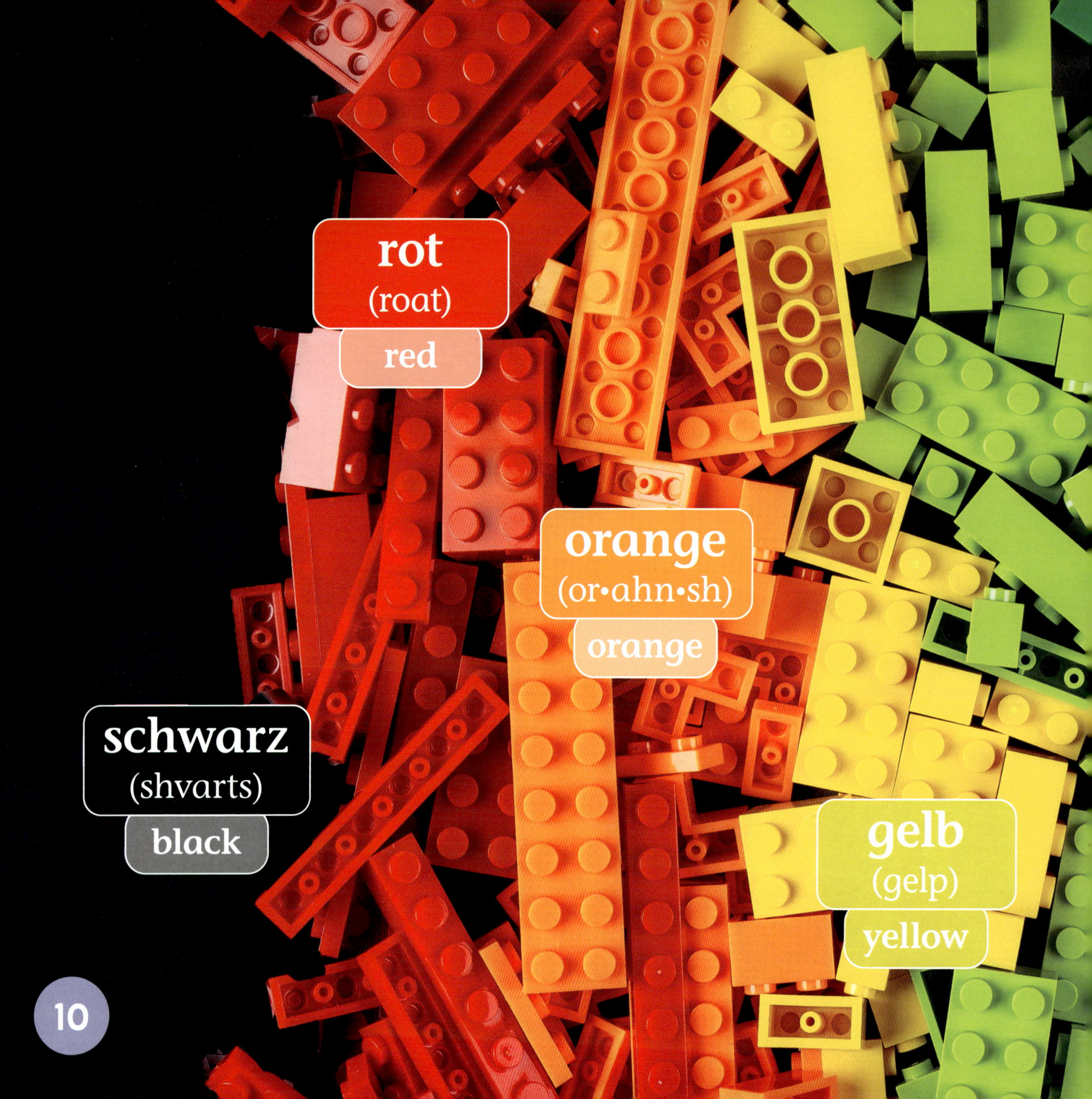
rot
(roat)
red
orange
(or•ahn•sh)
orange
schwarz
(shvarts)
black
gelb
(gelp)
yellow

grün
(groon)
green
die Farben
(far•ben)
the colors
blau
(bl•ow)
blue
weiß
(vice)
white
lila
(lee•la)
purple

hallo
(hal•lo)
hello

tschüss
(tchoos)
bye

guten Morgen
(goo•ten mor•gen)
good morning

gute Nacht
(goo•te nakt)
good night

bitte
(bit•teh)
please

danke
(dahn•ke)
thank you

ja
(ya)
yes

nein
(nine)
no

die Familie
(fa•mee•lee•ah)
the family

die Mutter
(mu•tehr)
mother

der Vater
(fah•tehr)
father

die Schwester
(shves•tehr)
sister

der Bruder
(brew•dehr)
brother

die Oma
(oh•ma)
grandma

der Opa
(oh•pa)
grandpa

die Tante
(tahn•te)
aunt

der Onkel
(ong•kel)
uncle

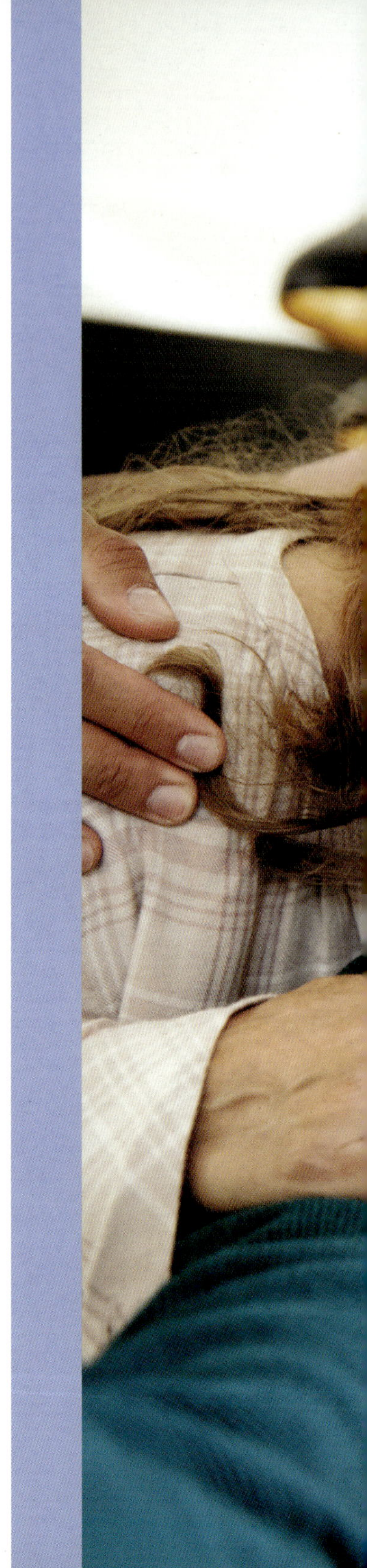

die Tiere
(teehr•e)
the animals
die Katze
(ka•tse)
cat

der Fisch
(fish)
fish
der Vogel
(foh•gel)
bird
der Hund
(hoo•nt)
dog

die Orte – The Places

das Haus
(haus)
house

die Schule
(shu•le)
school

der Park
(pahrk)
park

der Strand
(shtrahnt)
beach

das Alphabet – The Alphabet

letter	sound
A	ah
B	beh
C	tseh
D	deh
E	eh
F	eff
G	geh
H	haa
I	ee
J	yot
K	kah
L	el
M	em
N	en
O	oh
P	peh
Q	kuh
R	er
S	es
T	teh
U	uh
V	fow
W	veh
X	iks
Y	irp·se·lon
Z	tset
Ä	eeh
Ö	oeh
Ü	ueh
ß	ess·tset

Index